The Lake District is areas of outstanding many people who sl Amidst the greer grandeur, the angler and ordinary leisure seekers find peace of mind, far removed from the pressures and tensions of urban life.

Comprised in the counties of Lancashire, Westmorland and Cumberland, with an area of less than 900 square miles, the Lake District is a haven for anglers. Here the fisherman can enjoy his sport in truly magnificent surroundings.

Bob Patterson's interesting and well informed text is supported by a useful map, some black and white sketches and an impressive selection of first class colour illustrations of the area.

# contents

| | |
|---|---:|
| Map .. .. .. .. .. .. | 2 |
| The Fish of the Lake District .. .. .. .. | 3 & 4 |
| Requirements and Tackle .. .. .. .. | 5 |
| Bassenthwaite Lake .. .. .. .. .. | 6 |
| Brothers Water .. .. .. .. .. .. | 8 |
| Buttermere .. .. .. .. .. .. | 9 |
| Coniston Water .. .. .. .. .. .. | 11 |
| Crummock Water .. .. .. .. .. | 13 |
| Derwent Water .. .. .. .. .. .. | 15 |
| Elterwater .. .. .. .. .. .. | 17 |
| Ennerdale Water .. .. .. .. .. | 18 |
| Esthwaite Water .. .. .. .. .. | 19 |
| Grasmere .. .. .. .. .. .. .. | 20 |
| Haweswater .. .. .. .. .. .. | 21 |
| Loweswater .. .. .. .. .. .. | 22 |
| Rydal Water .. .. .. .. .. .. | 24 |
| Thirlmere .. .. .. .. .. .. | 25 |
| Ullswater .. .. .. .. .. .. | 26 |
| Wast Water .. .. .. .. .. .. | 28 |
| Watendlath Tarn .. .. .. .. .. | 30 |
| Windermere .. .. .. .. .. .. | 31 |

I

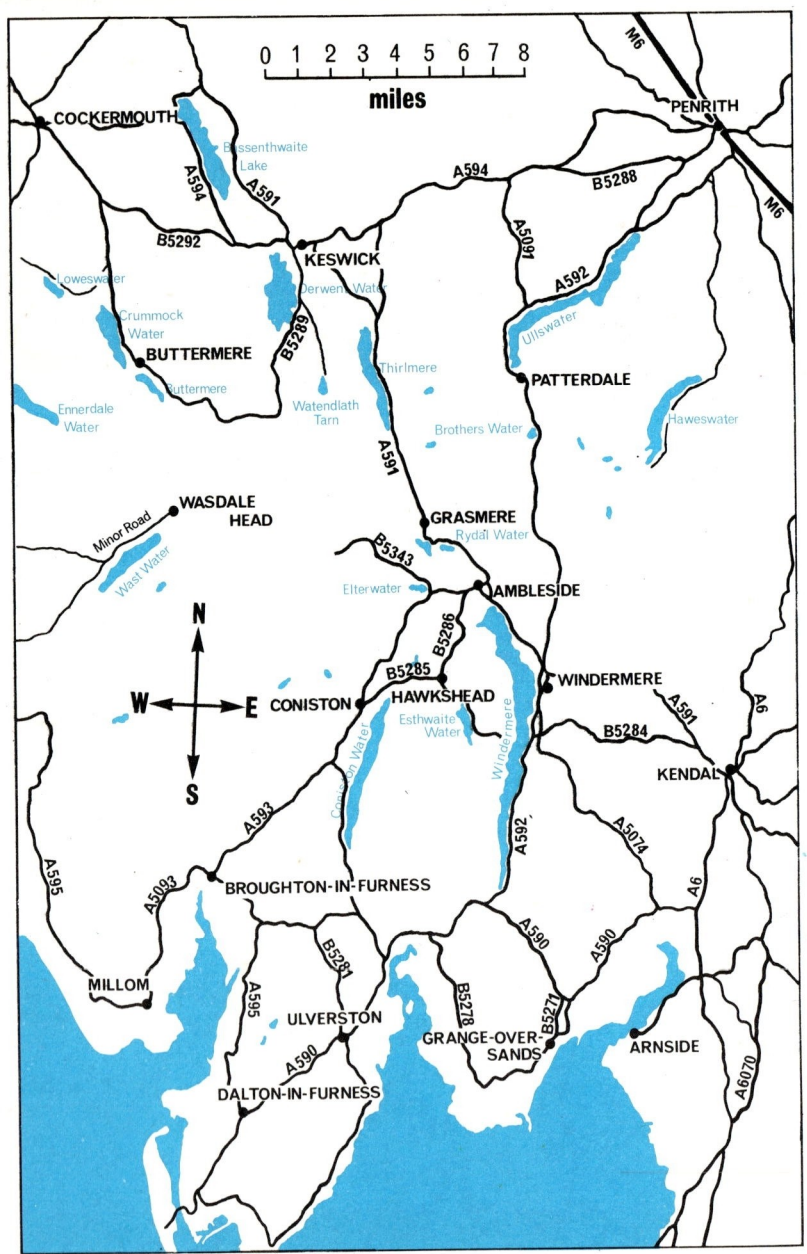

## PERCH (Perca fluviatilis)

Usually perch weigh up to 1 pound but 3 or 4 pound specimens can be caught. These little 'tigers' are indiscriminate feeders and are more common than any other fish in the Lakes. The larger perch are rather elusive and prefer to remain hidden in the deeper waters.

Baits: Maggots, worms, minnows (either dead or alive), and Devon minnow spinners are among the best baits known to the author. The finest fish ever landed were caught by using minnows.

## PIKE (Esox lucius)

This fierce predator weighs an average of ten pounds. Some monsters easily exceeding this figure may be caught. Pike are powerful killers and as loners their marauding exploits are concentrated around the warm, weedy shallows during the summer months. In the colder weather, pike can be sought in the deep pools and trenches.

Baits: Pike can be landed using dead herring, perch (either alive or dead), large minnow spinners, spoons or plugs.

## SALMON (Salmo salar)

It would be unfair to tag an average size and weight on the salmon, which is not as widely dispersed throughout the region as are most other species. Salmon are noble fighters and most of the runs are in association waters where weekly or daily permits are available at a reasonable cost, covering Wast Water, Bassenthwaite Lake and the River Derwent.

Baits: Spinners, spoons and flies are the time-tested methods of capture.

**COMMON**

**LAKE**

**BROWN**

**SEA**

**TROUT (Salmo trutta)**

The trout is a great fish, both beautiful in appearance and swift in movement. For the game fisherman it is a courageous fighter and is also a superb fish for the table. Heavyweight specimens are generally found in the main rivers and lakes, but the average weight is around 2 pounds. Smaller fish abound in the scattered becks and tarns. Their colours and feeding habits vary enormously, depending upon local conditions.

### Restrictions
Offal, cheese and salmon roe are prohibited baits throughout the Lake District. Maggots are banned as hookbait and groundbait during the coarse fish close season on Windermere, Grasmere, Rydal Water and Coniston Water.

### Requirements and Tackle
Permits must be obtained by anglers intending to fish in most of the waters in the Lake District. Details concerning the availability of permits are included in the chapters detailing the respective waters.

### Tackle
The tackle listed below covers the types of fishing most likely to be encountered. A beginner is advised to start with a seven-foot spinning rod, reel, spinners, line, hooks, floats, shot and a keep net.

### Rods
7 or 8 foot spinning
Fly
10 foot (all purpose)
Appropriate reels.

### Spinners and Spoons
Devon Minnows, Colorado and Kidney.

### Plugs
Divers and risers, jointed sinkers.

### Floats
Quill, Bob and Antennae. Also a pike float.

The following will complete the list: hooks, flies (wet and dry), landing net, pair of waders, gaff, line (various strains), split shot, bait tins, tackle box and Ordnance Survey maps. A wise angler would, of course, equip himself with a really good waterproof!

Please honour the *Country Code* and always seek advice if you are uncertain about fishing restrictions and permits. Land boundaries are apt to change from time to time, so you should endeavour not to trespass.

# Bassenthwaite Lake

Western shore reached via A594, eastern shore via A591.
Length 4 miles, breadth 1,300 yards, depth 70 feet.

Bassenthwaite is the most northerly of all the lakes, situated between Lord's Seat on the west and with Skiddaw towering high above the eastern shore. Not only is it one of the most beautiful lakes but it also offers a wealth of sport for anglers. The western shore is easily accessible and there are also good parking facilities. The eastern lakeside is harder to reach and much of it is privately owned. It can be reached from either Scarness or Broadness and the trek across the fields is well worth while for the excellent pike that are to be caught in Scarness and Broadness Bays.

From the A594, the western shore can be reached by descending the steep slope, crossing the disused railway track and then continuing

on down towards the lake. After heavy, prolonged rain it may be difficult to reach some of the places along this side. One of the better bays can still be reached by setting off from the Swan Hotel, following the path through the woods and fields to the north. After about ten minutes of steady walking one reaches an excellent spot for pike fishing in a wide, sweeping bay, fringed by weeds. The bed of the lake is reasonably free from snags. The northern end of the lake, near the Ouse Bridge is a good position for trout and salmon during the season. Boats may be hired from the Piel Wyke landing.

**Trout** – Fishing has improved since the lake was restocked. They frequent the deeper waters and estuaries. Good specimens have been taken using both Devon and line minnows.

**Pike** – are plentiful, lurking in the weedy shallows of the lake.

**Perch** – in most parts of the lake and numerous.

**Eels** – not very common, inhabiting the sandy pools.

**Vendace** – restricted to the deeper waters and very difficult to catch. Dead fish are occasionally washed ashore. Vendace are also found in Derwent Water and Loch Maben, Scotland.

**Permits** – available from the Leconfield Estate Company. Seasonal, weekly or day tickets are obtainable from the fisheries manager at Cockermouth Castle, the boathouse at Piel Wyke or from Temple's, Main Street, Keswick.

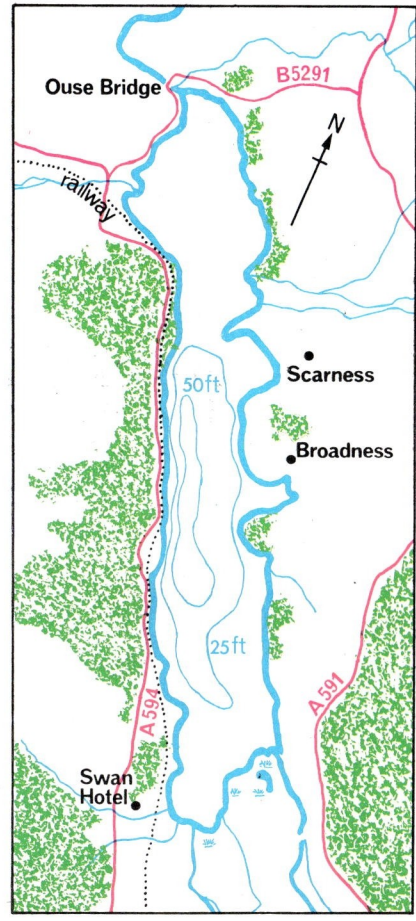

# Brothers Water

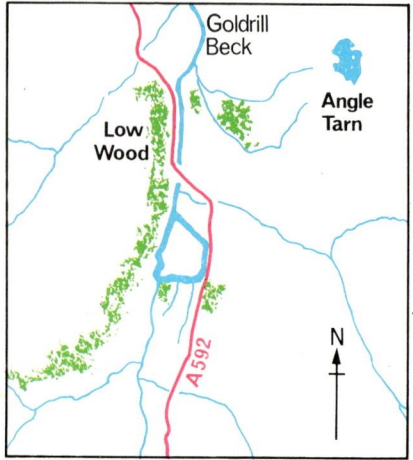

South via the A592 from Glenridding (Ullswater) for approximately 4 miles.
Length 560 yards, breadth 440 yards, depth 50 feet.

This is a small, remote lake situated in a 'U' shaped valley which joins Ullswater to the north. The spectacular Kirkstone Pass lies to the south of the valley, along the main road connecting Ullswater and Brothers Water.
The eastern shore can easily be reached from the road but the wooded western shore has to be journeyed on foot.
Goldrill Beck is a small meandering stream.

**Trout** – tend to be small in size although they are plentiful.

**Perch** – are not too easy to catch.

**Permits** – at the time of writing are not required. The property is owned by The National Trust.

# Buttermere

Approached from Keswick via Portinscale. Alternative route through Borrowdale and Honister Pass along the B5289.

Length 1¼ miles, breadth 670 yards, depth 94 feet.

Situated amidst magnificent scenery, Buttermere has a perfect setting of steep grey crags, waterfalls and conifer forests. The B5289 passes close to the eastern shore with the imposing screes of High Snockrigg in the background. Across the lake we look towards High Stile (2,649 feet) reflected into the blue-green waters which appear bottomless on a summer's day.

The surrounding heights may impose problems for the angler on a windy day, causing disturbing blasts across the surface of the lake. On a recent visit, fishing in the bay near Gatesgarth, a tremendous storm blew up from nowhere. The tiny white beach became engulfed in a sandstorm whilst the waves lashed against the shore. This bay holds good perch, and farther north is a very deep trench where weighty trout have been caught by spinning.

Along the eastern shore, I suggest

that you concentrate on the gravelly shallows where good results from either flies or spinners are possible. Spinning at a speed takes the best fish.

The northern end of the lake has proved most successful. Cars can be parked in Buttermere village and a short walk across the floor of the valley reaches Sour Milk Ghyll and its waterfalls. A further hundred yards down the lake, beneath Burtness Wood is a spot where excellent perch lurk, and a little further on good trout are to be found.

**Trout** – are plentiful and extremely delicious.

**Perch** – less numerous in Buttermere but are generally good sized.

**Permits** – available at the Bridge Hotel, Buttermere. The lake is owned by The National Trust who have several boats available for hire.

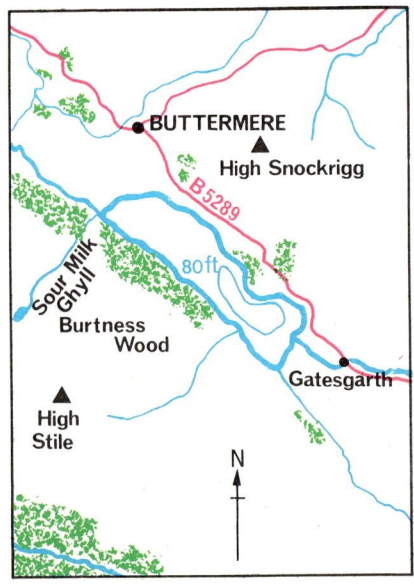

# Coniston Water

Approached from Ambleside along the A593.
Length 5½ miles, breadth 870 yards, depth 184 feet.

Both sides of the lake are beautifully wooded. The southern end of Coniston provides the better bays and the head of the lake the finer scenery. Both Peel Island and Fir Island are wooded. The minor road on the eastern side runs parallel to the lake and affords excellent access to the shore.

There are many species of fish in Coniston for which most of the methods previously mentioned provide good results. Spinning has not kidded many trout, but I have been successful when baiting with a lively brandling. Those who are proficient in the art of fly fishing should make good catches, especially when fishing at Oxen

House Bay where the A5084 skirts the western shore.

Although some people say that there are too many pike in Coniston any pike fishermen will find the sport excellent.

**Pike** – are both plentiful and large. Spinning is better than live or dead baiting, and large colorado spoons are the most effective. The best results are obtained from a boat.

**Perch** – are numerous, weighing on average about one pound. The best bait is either bunched maggots or juicy brandlings.

**Eels** – to be found in the deeper pools, are plentiful.

**Char** – very rare and best caught by trolling the deeper parts of the lake.

**Trout** – weigh up to one pound and are common. Worm or fly are ideal baits since spinning does not catch trout in the deeper waters.

**Permits** – are available in Coniston and boats may be hired on the lake.

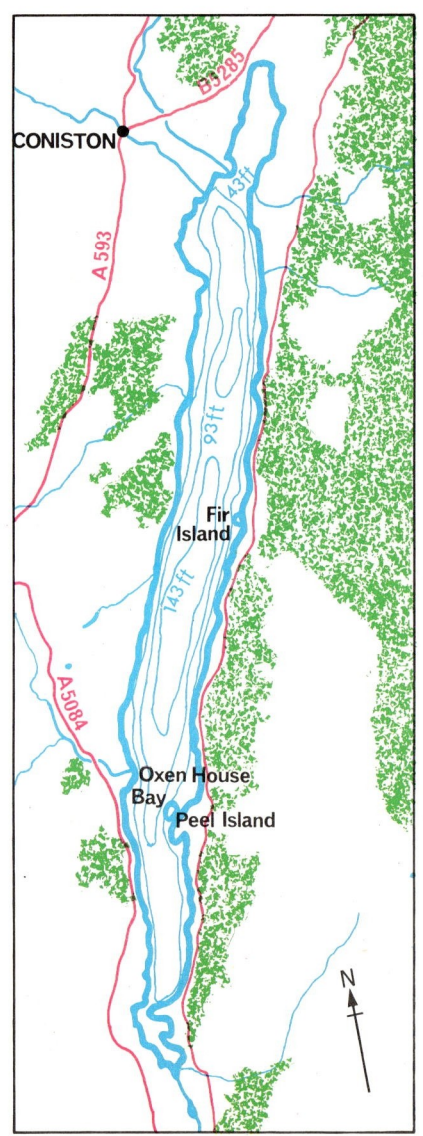

# Crummock Water

One mile from Buttermere along the B5289.
Length 2½ miles, breadth 1,000 yards, depth 144 feet.

Crummock Water is a beautiful lake set in the same valley as Buttermere, to which it was once joined. The roughness of Mellbreak and Ling Crags to the west and the mighty Grasmoor to the east is broken only by the smooth expanse of the lake.

The only wooded area is at the head of the lake, on the eastern shore. Elsewhere the beaches are pebbled.

The western shore may be reached on foot, either from Buttermere or Loweswater, and the trek beneath Mellbreak is well worth while. In some places, the bed of the lake falls away sharply, leaving many of the deep trenches and pools within easy reach of the shore. This is essentially a lake for game

fishermen, and provides sport for trout, salmon and sea trout. Perch are also here, but not in large numbers. Unfortunately, I know of no pike ever being caught in the lake.

Excellent trout have been taken from the shore below Mellbreak, especially from the point below Ling Crags. The shallows along the eastern shore should be sought by spinnermen who are after trout.

Based at Rannerdale you should not be disappointed as you fish for your supper.

**Salmon** – travel through the lake between April and November. Spinning is usually better than fly.

**Trout** – are fine fighters and extremely tasty. They are found in most parts of the lake. Fly fishing brings good results. Spinning in the shallow waters. Tackle the heavier fish by trolling a Devon minnow.

**Sea Trout** – in the river Cocker, near where it leaves the lake. Spinning with small spoons is the best method.

**Char** – lurk in the depths, 50 feet or more, so trolling is best using a shiny gold lure.

**Perch** – are not common and tend to be smaller than those of Bassenthwaite.

**Permits** – should be obtained from The National Trust, who own the lake. In addition, the usual local Fishery Board licence is required and may be obtained from Netherclose Farm, above Scalehill Bridge (on the Loweswater side) or at the Bridge Hotel, Buttermere, or Temple's, Keswick. Boats for hire are available.

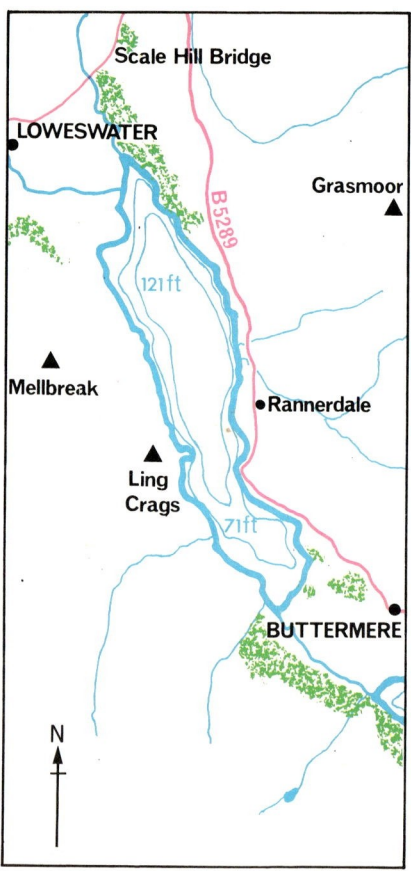

# Derwent Water

Western shore via Portinscale, eastern shore via B5289.
Length 3 miles, breadth $1\frac{1}{4}$ miles, depth 72 feet.

Derwent Water is in one of the loveliest of settings, offering first class amenities for anglers. The lake is also very popular with tourists, so the angler needs to search for the quieter places.

Friar's Crag, on the eastern shore, has given the author good-sized perch. The best results are when spinning with Devon minnow. The bottom of the lake tends to be rather rough and tackle may be lost if a slow rewind is employed.

Further along the bay, past Derwent Isle, it is possible to tussle with sizeable pike. However, much of the eastern shore skirts very shallow water and the sport is not as good as on the western side, especially

at Derwent Bay and Hawse End.

I recommend Great Bay at the southern end of the lake where some good pike are to be found. After parking the car off the B5289, there is some marsh land to cross. In dry weather it is a fairly easy route, following the wooden planks set in the marsh, but after heavy rain, it becomes impassable. The best bait to use here is perch – either alive or dead – which can be obtained from the waters to the left of the bay where the shoreline is quite rocky.

The River Derwent flows out of the lake into Bassenthwaite and is an ideal venue for night fishing. Some stretches are fished exclusively by local angling clubs.

**Trout** – mostly in the deeper waters, and caught by trolling. Good specimens have been taken with a fly, offered from a boat moored a little distance offshore either from Derwent Isle or Saint Herbert's Island.

**Pike** – are slightly declining in numbers although large creatures have been sighted in the north and south bays of the lake. Spinning has produced good fish in the northern waters, but either live or dead baiting is more successful in the south.

**Vendace** – restricted to the deeper waters, rarely coming to the lake side, making these fish rather difficult to capture.

**Permits** – for the lake are obtainable from Temple's, Main Street, Keswick, who also have information pertaining to the local fishing boundaries. Boats can be hired on the lake.

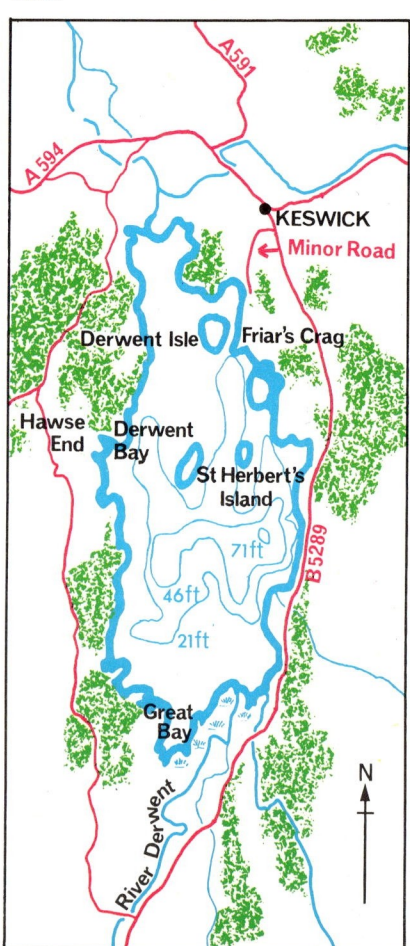

# Elterwater

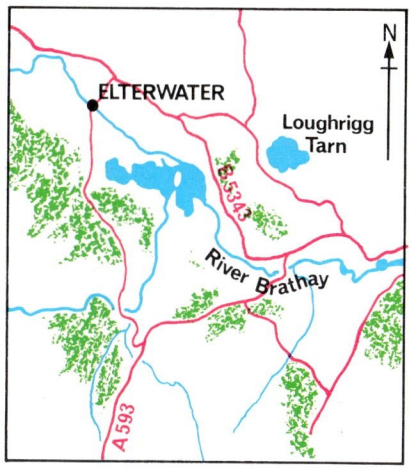

Three miles west of Ambleside along the A593 then via the B5343. Length 1,000 yards, breadth 300 yards, depth 20 feet.

This small but beautiful lake involves a considerable amount of walking to reach its shores. It is, understandably, a popular beauty spot with its richly wooded forests standing peacefully before the rugged Langdales.

It is unfortunate that the lake, being relatively shallow, lacks any serious sport although both trout and perch are to be found. Windermere is linked to Elterwater along the River Brathay and the Great Langdale Beck links up with numerous becks and tarns. Loughrigg Tarn is just $\frac{1}{2}$ a mile away to the east.

**Trout and Perch** – do not offer a great deal of sport.

**Permits** – enquiries should be made in Ambleside.

# Ennerdale Water

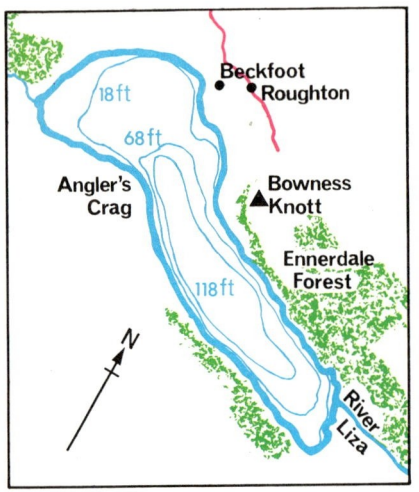

## ENNERDALE WATER

Follow the A5086 south of Cockermouth for four miles, turning left at Hodyoad on to the minor road to Roughton and Beckfoot. The north side of the lake is reached by a rough road.

Length $2\frac{1}{2}$ miles, breadth 1,000 yards, depth 148 feet.

Ennerdale Water is extremely difficult to reach but is well worth the effort. The southern shore can only be reached on foot. It is a beautiful, peaceful lake with a fine blend of surrounding crags and forests. The river Liza, in Ennerdale Forest, has good trout but is covered by private concerns. The lake does not hold any perch or pike but is well stocked with trout, particularly offshore at Bowness Knott. The lake is at its best between July and early September.

**Char** – are rare and inhabit only the deeper waters of the lake.

**Trout** – found everywhere and are best taken using the fly and spin methods.

**Permits** – from the Leconfield Trust at Cockermouth Castle.

# Esthwaite Water

From Ambleside via the A593 then the B5286 through Hawkshead along the eastern shore. A minor road gives access to the western shore.

Length 1½ miles, breadth 630 yards, depth 47 feet.

This delightful lake is small but offers a wealth of sport. It is surrounded by heavily wooded hillsides that lie between Coniston Water and Windermere, to which it is connected by Cunsey Beck.

If you are after game fish such as trout, the gravelly shallows are the best locations. The species found here are wonderfully coloured and their pink flesh is delicious to eat.

Unfortunately, pike are not very common but may be found in the bays at the southern end of the lake. Perch also thrive there and can be taken with a baited worm or minnow.

At the head of the lake, a fish less common in the lakes has established itself in the deep pools around Priest Pot – the roach.

One of the best places for eels is in Cunsey Beck, near the aptly named Eel House.

**Trout** – are pink-fleshed and plentiful.

**Pike** – decreasing in numbers.

**Roach** – recently introduced and found mostly at Priest Pot.

**Eels** – are abundant, especially in Cunsey Beck.

**Permits** – available from either the Post Office at Hawkshead, or from Esthwaite Estates Limited, who also have boats for hire.

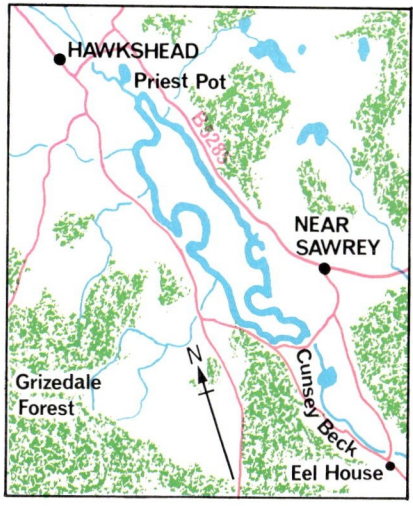

# Grasmere

From Ambleside via the A591.
Length 1 mile, breadth 730 yards, depth 70 feet.

This tranquil little lake is fed by the River Rothay at its head and linked with Rydal Water to the south. Access to the western shore is good. Surrounded by imposing fells, the lake has many literary associations which make it a favourite haunt of both artists and photographers. It is, however, less popular with anglers.

Trout are found in the deeper waters below 30 feet, but are difficult to catch. As in most of the lakes, perch are common but in Grasmere they tend to be small in size.

The walk from the road below Huntingstile is quite difficult, but once the lakeside is reached you should be able to catch some good sized perch, using live-baited minnows. Pike have been caught by using a green-back, yellow-belly minnow spinner. At the point called the Wyke, trout weighing about half a pound have been taken.

**Trout** – not very common.

**Pike** – few in numbers.

**Perch** – plentiful.

**Permits** – issued by the Lowther Estates and available in Grasmere village.

# Haweswater

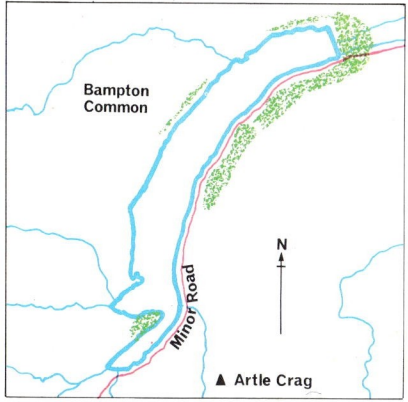

Along the A6 from Penrith, turning right at Long Cairn along minor road through Newtown, Askham and Bampton and along the eastern shore of the reservoir.

Length 4 miles, breadth $\frac{1}{2}$ mile, depth 200 feet.

Haweswater is the most easterly lake and one of the more difficult to reach. The south-eastern side is flanked by a minor road but the south-western shore can only be reached by a footpath. No longer a lake, Haweswater is now a reservoir, owned by Manchester Waterworks, who raised the water level by 90 feet.

Fishing is limited and permission should be obtained in writing from the Manchester Waterworks Committee, Town Hall, Manchester. Boats are not available on these waters.

# Loweswater

From Keswick along the A594 and then on the B5292 to High Lorton. Take the B5289 towards Crummock Water, turn first right into Loweswater village and then on towards the lake.

Length 1 mile, breadth 586 yards, depth 53 feet.

Loweswater is a small, remote lake situated in the same valley as Crummock Water and Buttermere. From Cockermouth, Loweswater may be reached via the A5086. The north eastern shore is easily approached by road but the opposite side is only accessible by footpath.

Despite the considerable journey involved, Loweswater is a lake that is well worth visiting, especially on an early June or July morning around 7 a.m. when the mist has dispersed.

Just beneath Holme Wood is an ideal position where trout, pike and perch eagerly feed. You can hit good pike offshore from Waterend, at the head of the lake. Early morning fishermen are sure to catch good trout in fine weather with a small kidney spoon.

The lake is full of perch, which, although not in the heavyweight class, are extremely tasty. Many people are not aware of perch as a table fish, but when grilled or lightly fried in some butter, they are absolutely delicious. Make the shore between Watergate Farm and Highcross your base and you will be well rewarded when worm fishing.

**Trout** – are abundant but the superior fish are found in the deepest waters. Silver spoons are more suitable than Devon minnows.

**Pike** – also numerous, mostly found lurking in the weedy shallows. Spin slowly on this lake.

**Perch** – can be found in most parts of the lake.

**Salmon** – should be in fairly good runs a little way out from Highcross.

**Permits** – obtainable at the Bridge Hotel, Buttermere, the Kirkstile Inn, Loweswater, or Temple's, Keswick.

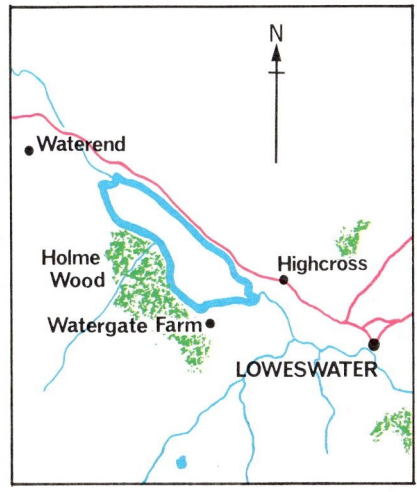

# Rydal Water

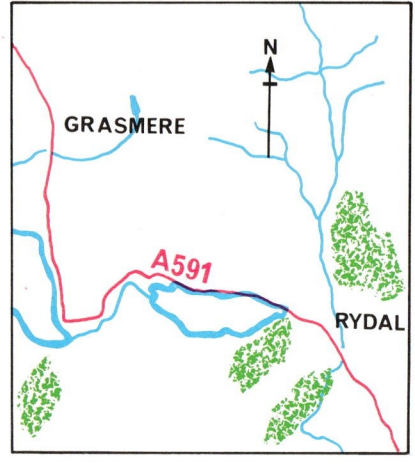

Two miles from Ambleside along the A591.
Length ¾ mile, breadth 370 yards, depth 56 feet.

Rydal Water is a beautiful little lake linked with Grasmere and Windermere. It is owned by a private association from whom a permit should be obtained. Both trout and perch can be found but this picturesque lake is perhaps better left to the sight-seers.

**Permits** – can be obtained locally in Ambleside.

# Thirlmere

Can be approached from Keswick via the A591 or from Ambleside along the same road going north.

Length 3½ miles, breadth 704 yards, depth 153 feet.

Thirlmere was originally two lakes until the level was raised by 50 feet, making a reservoir for the city of Manchester. It is in a beautiful setting, nestling beneath the mighty heights of Helvellyn. Magnificent forests, waterfalls and wooded islands combine to create an ideal place for the photographer but not for the angler. Fishing is restricted and permission must be obtained in writing from the Manchester Waterworks Department, Town Hall, Manchester. Pike and perch are plentiful.

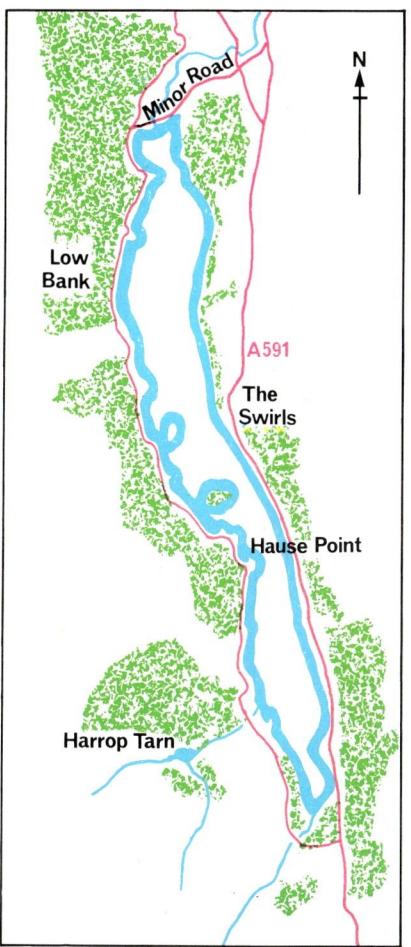

# Ullswater

From Penrith, via the A592.
Length 7½ miles, breadth 1,100 yards, depth 205 feet.

Ullswater, its fells and its fishing can only be described as majestic. The author has fished in all seasons and conditions, but finds August to be the best time. The A592 follows the north-western side of the lake and a minor road through Pooley Bridge affords access to parts of the south-eastern shore.

Howtown, on the road to Martindale is close to a pier and some pleasant shoreline at Waternook. The wide sweeping bay offers fine trout, particularly on a fine day. Many anglers consider Ullswater to hold the best trout, which may not be necessarily true, although they do have a certain greatness. Further along the shore, just past the Mountain Rescue Post at Sandwick is another superb place for trout, where the becks of Boredale, Bannerdale and Ramsgill enter the lake.

On the opposite side, near the A592 and A5091 junction is Aira Point, off which the water is deep, making an ideal place for spinning.

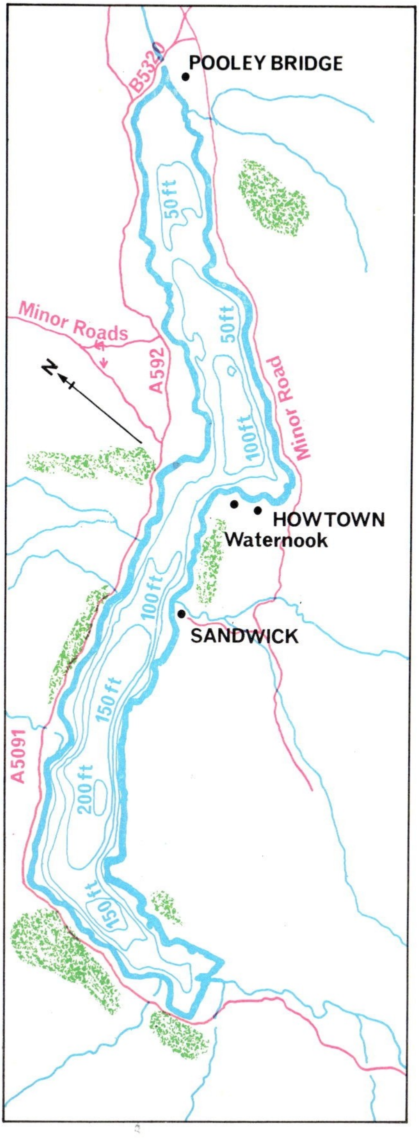

The lake's southern end teems with very good perch, although some of my best examples have been caught further up towards Pooley Bridge.

It is well worth hiring one of the boats available and the results will far surpass those of the shore fishermen.

**Trout** – are both good and tasty. Spinning is better in the deeper stretches of water.

**Perch** – are of good quality and plentiful.

**Permits** – are available from Temple's, Keswick, or Wilkinson's & Sykes, Penrith.

27

# Wast Water

From Ambleside along the A593. Turn right after Skelwith Bridge through Wrynose and Hard Knott Passes to Santon Bridge. Turn right for the lake.

Length 3 miles, breadth 880 yards, depth 260 feet.

Wast Water is the most remote of all the lakes within a terrain that is

both rugged and spectacular. Only the north–western shore is approached by road.

Despite the difficult journey, a visit to this lake is well worth while. The southern end is bordered by rich forests and fragrant gardens, while the famous steep screes descend sharply to the south-eastern shore. The grandeur of Wast Water with the heights of Yewbarrow, Kirk Fell, Great Gable and the Scafell Pikes, is breathtaking.

Wast Water is rich in game fish, the best month being July. This is the deepest English lake. The water becomes deep quite close to the shore, where the big fish are within easy reach.

A footpath at the head of the lake leads to Wasdale Head Hall Farm. This is one of the many places where good sized trout are taken. Most of the western shore offers excellent fishing facilities, especially within the small bays about a mile from Wasdale Hall. Salmon are known to congregate a little way out from where Over Beck enters the lake, below Bowderdale.

**Char** – are mainly in the deeper waters.

**Trout** – plentiful and weighing on average from 3 to 4 pounds.

**Salmon and Sea Trout** – both are very good. Employ the slow and then fast spinning method. The nearby river Irt which flows out of the lake is also excellent. Greendale and Low Tarns have plenty of trout worth trying for.

**Permits** – should be obtained from the Leconfield Trust at Cockermouth Castle.

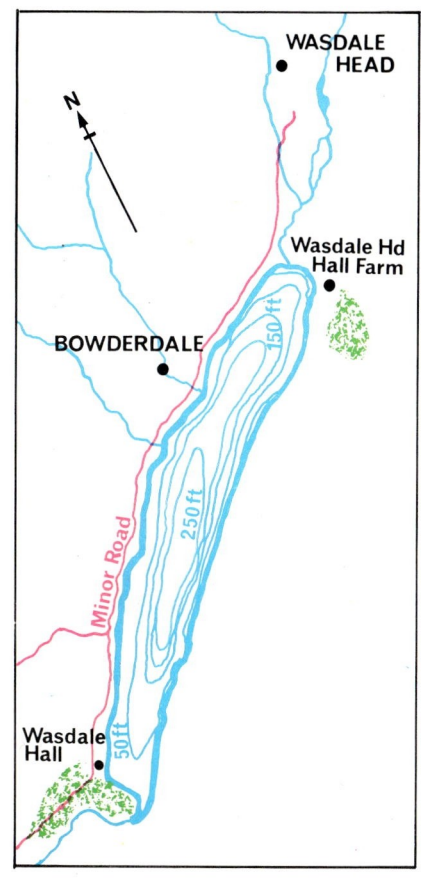

# Watendlath Tarn

The B5289 from Keswick, past Derwent Water, turning left just before Barrow Bay.

Watendlath is a small hamlet on the edge of the tarn and has good parking facilities. Although this is one of the few tarns referred to in this book, many others are worth visiting. Watendlath tarn is not particularly deep and the perch are mainly small in size, but it is said to hold a pike of record-breaking proportions! It is possible that the growth of the colony of perch is actually being stunted by a large predator. In a bar in Keswick, an elderly gentleman told an amusing story of how he had seen the big pike of Watendlath. As the night wore on, the size of the fish increased alarmingly in size, leaving one more uncertain than ever!

The author has weathered many dirty days dreaming and trying for it without success. A mystery perhaps, but who knows?

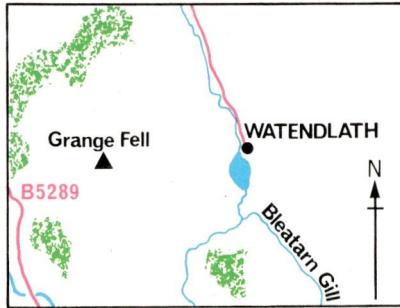

# Windermere

From Kendal, Ambleside or Keswick via the A594.
Length 10½ miles, breadth 1,610 yards, depth 219 feet.

Windermere is the largest and supposedly the "Queen of the Lakes", although it is not really a mountain lake, being surrounded by thickly-wooded hills. The lake is unfortunately too commercialised, and the angler must accept the fact that much of the best fishing has to be reached by boat.

The A592 offers good access to the eastern shore. Much of the western side is bordered by private grounds and the minor road only passes the shore in a few places. Good pike lurk around Belle Isle and boats may be hired nearby. Good trout have been taken in the waters near Wray Castle on the western shore.

The southern end of the lake, near

31

where the river Leven enters, is a venue for excellent perch fishing. The larger fish have taken any baits offered to them. Just south of the ferry landing, on the western side, is Bryers Fold, offering excellent perch and trout fishing. When you fish Windermere, particularly by boat, you will discover many other good swims for yourself as you explore these waters.

**Perch** – are teeming in numbers and found in most of the usual places.

**Trout** – plentiful. The larger fish are taken by spinning a slow spoon in deeper waters, but faster where shallow.

**Pike** – very good, spinning with large bright lures.

**Char** – Windermere has quite a number of char. Odd catches are landed by deep-fished worms, but usually the trolling method is more successful.

**Permits** – are obtainable from the tackle shop in Bowness, which is about 200 yards from the piers, along the main street.

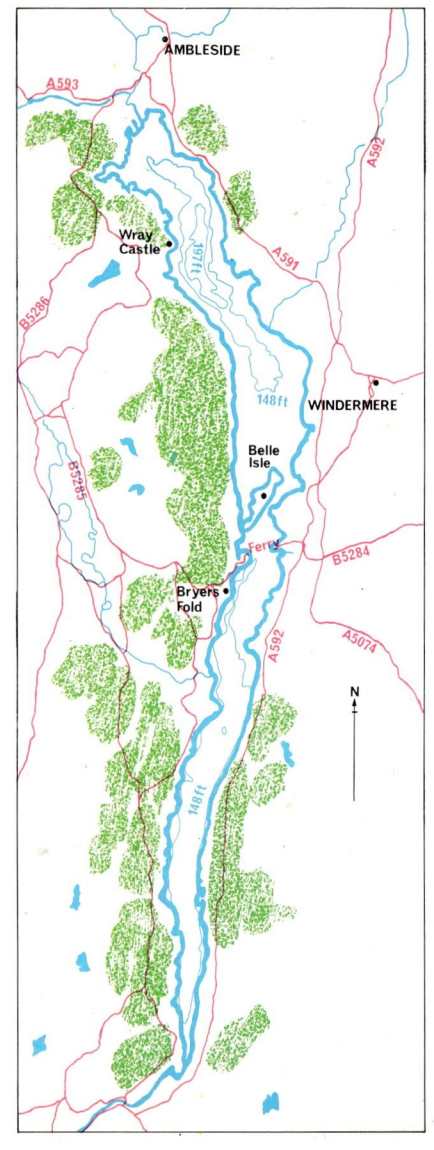